The Wonderful Stories of Jesus from the New Testament

BOOK TWO

DAYBREAK
PUBLISHERS

P.O. Box 261129 • San Diego, CA 92196

DB46202
ISBN 1-885358-18-0

BOOK TWO

Stories from Scripture
retold by

RACHEL HALL

SUSAN SAYERS

MARGARET JOY

JANE PORTER

ANNA MORRIS

HELEN ANDREWS

Illustrated by

ARTHUR BAKER

THE PALM TREE BIBLE
© 1996 Palm Tree Press

Published in the United States of America by
DAYBREAK PUBLISHERS
P.O. Box 261129 • San Diego, CA 92196

Printed in Hong Kong

Contents

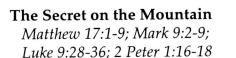

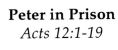
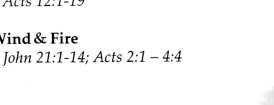

Jesus Gets Lost

Was it wrong of Jesus to wander off from His parents in Jerusalem? What do you think of His explanation that He had to do the work of His Father?

Long ago, in a village called Nazareth,
  there lived a happy family —
  a father, a mother and their son.

The father's name was Joseph.
  The mother was named Mary.
  And the son
  — yes, you've guessed —
  was Jesus.

They lived in peace with each other
  and with their neighbors.

Joseph was the village carpenter.
  He made all the sorts of things the people
  in the village needed:
  — feeding troughs for the animals
  — cribs for the new babies
  — tables and benches for the houses.
You think of it and Joseph made it!

And, of course, Jesus was always
  wanting to help Joseph.
  Like all children,
  He probably got in the way sometimes,
  but on the whole,
  He was a great help to Joseph.
  By the time He was 12,
  He had learned all about
  making things.

Each year everyone in the village,
  and in all the villages around,
  went to the big city called Jerusalem.

They went for one of the most important
  Jewish feasts
  — the feast of the Passover.*

*It is called "Passover" because during Moses'
time God "passed over" His people when He
sent the worst trouble. That story is found in
the book of Exodus, in the Old Testament.

They all gathered there to thank God
  for helping them to escape from
  the wicked king of Egypt years and
  years before.

Some walked,
  others rode on donkeys or camels,
  and others went by cart,
  but go they all did!

The men went in the front of
  the procession,
  and the women went behind.
  The children could go where they liked,
  and, of course,
  it was great fun for them.

When the villagers reached Jerusalem
  they went to the temple,
  Joseph, Mary and Jesus with them.

They loved the singing of the choir,
  and the seven silver trumpets which
  were always played on important feasts.
  And they loved the beautiful prayers
  thanking God for looking after them.

The Passover was a very special time.

8

Oh, dear!
Jesus was not with either of them.
What had happened to Him?

Of course, as soon as Mary and Joseph
found that Jesus was not with
either of them,
they made their way back to Jerusalem.
They were so worried about Jesus,
and they looked everywhere for Him:
up one street and down another,
in the shops, behind walls,
in fact, everywhere a boy might hide.

But Jesus was not hiding.

The villagers were not due to start
for home again for a few hours,
so Joseph, Mary and Jesus
decided to look around the shops.

They saw beautiful clothes,
colorful mats,
some very useful pots
and all sorts of delicious food.

Of course, being simple village people,
they were very impressed!

At last it was time for them all
to go home again.
Just as before, the procession lined up
— men in the front,
women at the back.

"Jesus must be with Mary,"
thought Joseph.
"Jesus must be with Joseph,"
thought Mary.

Never mind
  — perhaps they would find Jesus there.
  So Mary and Joseph
  joined the crowd.

Well, Jesus was certainly there
  in the temple.
  Not as one of the crowd, though.

He was with the Jewish
  teachers, called rabbis.
  What on earth was He doing there?

Just as they were beginning to
  give up hope of finding Jesus,
  Mary and Joseph noticed crowds
  making their way to the temple.

"That's funny,"
  they said to each other,
  "the Passover feast finished long ago.
  Why are all these people going
  back to the temple?"

"Why have You treated
us like this?"
she asked Jesus.
"Didn't You realize how worried
Your father and I would be?"

Jesus answered His mother kindly:
"Why did you worry so much?
You know I must do the work
of My Father in heaven."

But Mary and Joseph did not really
understand what He was talking about.

Well, believe it or not,
Jesus was answering
the rabbis' questions!
And the rabbis were astonished.
How could a boy of only 12
know so much
about God and
about the way God wants us to live?

We know the answer to that, don't we?
Because Jesus is the Son of God.
But the rabbis and the crowd
who listened in amazement didn't!

At last, Jesus finished talking
to the rabbis
and the crowd drifted away.
Mary was very proud of all
the things Jesus had said,
but she was also kind of angry.

Mary looked after the house
and cooked delicious meals.
Joseph spent his time in the
workshop sawing and hammering.
And Jesus loved and obeyed His parents.
He learned something new every day.
He was well liked by all the villagers,
and He grew closer and closer
to God, His Father.

Note:
This story is found in Luke 2:41-52.

Nevertheless,
Jesus did as His parents said,
and they all set off
back to Nazareth.

The other villagers were so glad
to see Jesus safe among them again.

Soon everything was back to normal
in the happy home of Nazareth.

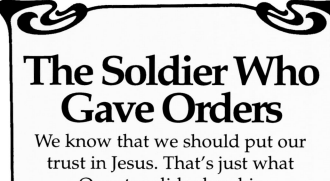

The Soldier Who Gave Orders

We know that we should put our trust in Jesus. That's just what Quentus did when his servant was ill.

"Good morning, sir!
Here are your sandals
and bath water,"
said Jeremy,
hoping he hadn't
spilled too much.

Quentus yawned and smiled.
"Ah, thank you, Jeremy,"
he said.
"You are learning to
be a good servant.
Now run along and
have your breakfast."

Jeremy trotted off happily.
He liked working
for his new master.
Quentus was strict,
but very kind.

In his soldier's uniform
Quentus looked really important,
because he was a centurion,
in charge of a hundred men.

But in bed he just looked
a bit like Jeremy's dad —
comfortable and whiskery.

That morning they set off
through their town,
Capernaum.

13

First stop was the synagogue.
 "Any problems?"
 asked Quentus.

"Just a small leak, sir,"
 said the builder.
 "Alex could fix it for us."

"Okay, Jeremy,"
 ordered Quentus,
 "run and get Alex.
 Tell him to come
 right away."

Jeremy was off
 like a rocket.
 "Yes, sir!"
 he shouted.

And sure enough,
 that leak was fixed
 in no time.

Jeremy's job was to
walk behind Quentus,
carrying things
or running messages.

Everyone bowed
 or waved to Quentus
 as they marched
 (and scampered) along.

Then the soldiers
had to be inspected.

Quentus barked orders
and they all obeyed.

"Atten…TION!"

"Forward…MARCH!"

"About…FACE!"

Jeremy would have liked
to join in.

Next they met a family
dancing in the street.

One woman danced
up to Quentus.
"Excuse me, sir,"
she gasped,
"but my daughter
has just had a baby son
and we're so happy."

"Well, congratulations!"
beamed Quentus.
"May I join in?"

"Of course,"
said everyone.

So Jeremy and Quentus
danced as well.

One day, Jeremy woke up
  in awful pain.
  He felt really ill
  and couldn't move at all.

Quentus came to see him.
  He bathed his head
  and made him
  more comfortable.

"Poor young Jeremy,"
  he said,
  "we must get you
  well again."

But Jeremy didn't get better.
  He got worse.
  Quentus paced up and down,
  looking sad.

Then he had an idea.
  A man named Jesus
  was visiting Capernaum
  that day and He was good
  at making people well.

Quentus saw Him
  in the distance
  and marched
  up to Him.

"I tell this man 'Come!'
    and he comes;
    I tell that man 'Go!'
    and he goes.

"Well, You have much more
    power than I have.
    I'm not important enough
    to have You visit my house,
    but if You just give the order, sir,
    I know my servant will be healed."

Jesus looked at him
    in amazement and delight.

"Do you know,"
    He said at last,
    "I have never met
    anyone who trusts Me
    so much, anywhere before —
    not even in Israel!"

"Sorry to bother You, sir,"
    he said to Jesus, "but my young servant
    can't move and is in terrible pain."

"Then I will heal him," said Jesus.

The people crowded around.
    "Yes, do help him, Jesus," they begged.

"This centurion is such a good man.
    He even built our synagogue!"

The centurion blushed
    and looked at the ground
    in embarrassment.

Then he cleared his throat.
    "Hmm hmm. Sir,
    I'm a soldier," he began,
    "so I'm used to giving orders.

17

Then Jesus turned
  to Quentus.

"You can go home now.
  Let your servant be healed,
  just as you believed
  he would be."

Quentus bowed politely,
  thanked Jesus,
  and marched home.

His march soon turned
  into a sprint —
  he couldn't wait
  to see Jeremy.

Just as he reached
  his doorway,
  Jeremy was bounding out,
  so they ran into each other,
  laughing and whooping
  with joy.

For Jeremy was
  just as strong
  and just as healthy
  as he had always been.

His illness had vanished.

Quentus lifted him
  high on his shoulders
  so he could see Jesus.

"There is the man who
  made you better, Jeremy,"
  said Quentus, gently.

"I trusted Him to heal you
  and He didn't let me down."

So together they walked
  to Jesus,
  to thank Him.

Note:
This story is found in Matthew 8:5-13 and
Luke 7:1-10.

Grandma Has a Fever

"You've made her better!" says Peter.
Perhaps we all have the power to
make other people better, by caring
for them and asking God to
make them well again.

It was a lovely sunny day.
Everyone felt glad to be alive.

Jesus went to the synagogue
with His friends, James and John,
and Andrew and Peter,
who were all fishermen.
They had tied up their boats,
because it was the Sabbath,
when they rested from work.

In the synagogue
they heard wonderful stories
about how God
looked after His people
every moment of their lives.

They sang some songs
to thank God for everything.
The friends came out of the synagogue
smiling and happy.

"All that singing has made me hungry,"
said James.

"Me, too," said his brother, John.

Peter laughed.
He knew what good appetites they had.
"Why don't you all come to our house
for a bite to eat?" he said.

"Great idea!" said James.
He knew there was always a good meal
at Peter's house.

"We'd love to," agreed John.

19

"And You, too, Jesus," said Peter.
 "Come and see where we live.
 Everyone in our family
 is longing to meet You."

"Yes," said Andrew,
 "we've told them so much about You."

"Especially Grandma," said Peter.
 "She's a nice old lady.
 She's always interested
 in everything we do.

"Grandma, can you make the meal stretch
 to three more?"
 he called.

"Just wait until you see
 who we've got with us!"

But there was no answer.

"And she loves meeting new people.
 She'll be thrilled to pieces
 if we bring You home for a meal."

"Yes, do come," said Andrew.

"Thank you," said Jesus,
 "I'd love to."

They strolled along near the Sea of Galilee
 to the house where Peter and Andrew
 lived with their family.

Outside were sails
 and lengths of fishing net
 hung out to dry on the wall.

Peter hurried ahead of the others.
 He was so happy
 that their friend Jesus
 was coming to their house for a meal.

He burst into the house.

The house was strangely quiet.

"Grandma! Grandma?"
  he called again.
  "We've brought someone special
  to meet you.
  It's someone
  you've been asking to see for ages!"

But there was still no answer.
  Peter began to feel frightened.

The servant girl came tiptoeing
  out of the side room.

She shut the door quietly behind her.
  "Thank goodness you're back,
  Master," she whispered.

"She fell sick all of a sudden,
  with a very high fever.
  We haven't been able
  to do anything to help her.
  Oh, what shall we do?"

Peter turned to his friends
  who had just come into the house.

His happy face looked pale and shocked.
  Grandma was a very old lady,
  and he loved her dearly.

"It's Grandma," he whispered.
  "She's got a high fever.
  Oh, Jesus, what shall we do?"

"Let Me see her," said Jesus.

Peter led the way to the side room.

He opened the door gently.
  Grandma was in bed.
  She looked so tiny and old
  lying there.
  Her face was wet with sweat,
  and she was trembling all over
  with fever.
  Her teeth were chattering;
  she was hot and then cold.

Peter had never seen her look so ill.
  Now he was really frightened.

He turned to his friend
  and said again,
  "Oh, Jesus, what shall we do?"

Jesus went over to the bed.

He bent over the old lady
  and took hold of her hand.

"Let Me help you up,"
  He said gently.

The old lady stopped trembling.

Her tiny body lay quiet
  for a moment.
  She opened her eyes.

Then she tightened her grip
  on Jesus' hand
  and sat up.

She pushed back the covers,
  put her feet down on the floor
  and stood up.

It was unbelievable!

Grandma looked around at the visitors crowding into the room and beamed.

"It's wonderful
  to have you all here," she said.
  "I will go get wine for you —
  and then I will bring you
  a delicious meal.
  This is going to be a real celebration!"

"It's one Sabbath
  I won't soon forget," said Peter.

"Nor I," said Grandma.

Note:
This story is found in
Matthew 8:14-17,
Mark 1:29-31 and
Luke 4:38-39.

"You've made her better!"
  exclaimed Peter.

He could hardly believe his eyes.

"Oh, Jesus, thank You!"

He gave Grandma a great big hug.
  He was very fond of her!

The old lady smiled up at Jesus.

"Welcome," she said.
  "I'm sorry I wasn't able
  to meet You at the door.
  I suddenly began feeling
  very sick indeed.

"But now I feel better
  than I have for years!
  You must all sit down.
  I'll soon have
  some water and towels ready for you.
  Your feet must be dusty!"

The Wild Man in the Desert

Even people who are mentally ill can get better when they are loved and understood.

The city was busy as usual.

At the market, people bought bright coats, pottery and chickens; others chose vegetables, combs and cloth.

The children played by the well, and old granddads sat in the shade chatting together.

Suddenly, there was shouting and crashing coming from one of the city streets.

A mother came racing among the stalls, clutching her baby.

"Abdeel has escaped again!" she cried. And you never saw a market empty so fast!

24

"It's no good,"
  said Susan.
  "He isn't safe enough
  to live in our city."

"He'll have to live
  out in the desert
  with the pigs,"
  suggested Marilyn.

"Won't he be lonely?"
  asked little Laura.

"That can't be helped,"
  said the others.

Poor Abdeel
  was very ill —
  not in his body,
  but in his mind.

You see, Satan and his demons
  lived in Abdeel.
  Sometimes they made him wild.
  He would break his chains
  and charge through the city.

Nothing was safe,
  so everyone was terrified.
  They peeked out
  as he pounded past
  into the desert.

So, this time,
  nobody went to bring Abdeel back.

25

One day
    Abdeel was gazing out
    over the sea,
    when he saw a boat
    sail up to the beach —
    his beach.

Abdeel's mind
    felt danger.
    He picked up stones
    to throw at the strangers
    in the boat
    and scare them off.

The strangers were
    Jesus and His friends.

But when Jesus
    climbed ashore
    and started to walk
    up the beach,
    Abdeel put his stones down.
    Somehow, he didn't want
    to throw them now.

His clothes were soon
    filthy and in shreds,
    and he lived among the caves.

In his wild fits
    he would moan and scream,
    and throw himself against rocks.

But the people
    were too frightened
    to help him.

Jesus took Abdeel's hands
and looked straight into
his eyes.

He knew that the demons
had taken over
Abdeel's mind,
and He wanted to
clear them all away
to make him well.

"What is your name?"
He asked.

Suddenly he felt
loved and understood.

So he ran,
jumping over the rocks
and stones as he went,
until he reached Jesus
and knelt at His feet.

"I-I-I know
who You are!"
he stammered.
"You are J-J-Jesus,
the Son of God."

The demons answered
  for Abdeel.

"Oh, there are lots of us!"
  they said.

Abdeel felt as if
  light was spreading through him,
  until his mind
  was bright and clear.

He remembered
  who he was!
  The world did not seem
  terrifying any more!

And the whole herd
  of pigs,
  now possessed by the demons,
  suddenly dashed straight
  into the sea.

When the people from the city
  saw Jesus and Abdeel
  chatting together
  like old friends
  they couldn't believe
  their eyes!

"Look — that's Abdeel!"
  shouted Laura.

"It can't be,"
  said the others.

(But it was!)

"But please don't send us
far away. Send us
into the pigs over there."

"All right," said Jesus,
  and He prayed over Abdeel.

"I need you here,"
  Jesus said.
  "Will you do a job for Me?"

Abdeel's eyes shone.
  "Of course, Jesus,
  I'll do ANYTHING!"

"Then tell everyone here
  about how God
  made you well.
  Then perhaps
  they will believe in Him."

So, happy and free,
  Abdeel ran off
  to start his important job.

Note:
This story is found in
Matthew 8:28-34,
Mark 5:1-20 and
Luke 8:26-39.

They were rather scared
  of Jesus' great power,
  and asked Him to go away.

Jesus looked at them sadly
  as He got into the boat.

"Hey, wait for me!"
  shouted Abdeel.
  "Please let me come
  with You."

Jesus grinned
  and put His arm
  around Abdeel.

Jesus on the Sea

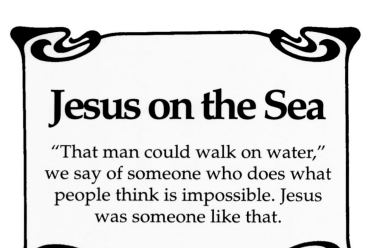

"That man could walk on water," we say of someone who does what people think is impossible. Jesus was someone like that.

In Israel there is a big lake
  called the Sea of Galilee.

It is a very beautiful place
  set among the hills
  with clear, fresh water.

Mostly it is very calm and quiet.

But sometimes it isn't a bit calm.
  Sudden winds whip up the water
  until the waves rage wild and high.

And when that happens,
  wise fishermen head for home!

Jesus knew the lake well;
  some of His best friends
  were fishermen.

He had met Peter and Andrew,
  James and John while they were busy
  mending their nets.

"Peter," said Jesus
  one warm evening,
  "can we sail over
  to the other side today?"

"Yes, of course, Lord,"
  said Peter.
  "Hop in."

One wave crashed right into the boat,
  and James and Andrew had to bail out
  water as fast as they could.

"Trim the sail!"
  "Turn her into the wind!"
    "Bail faster!"
  Everyone was shouting.

James looked across at Jesus.
  "Good gracious!" he thought,
  "Jesus is still asleep!"

"WAKE UP, JESUS, WAKE UP!
  We're in danger of drowning,
  and we need Your help!"

Jesus climbed aboard
  and sat down in the boat.

James and John pushed
  the strong boat out,
  before leaping in themselves.

Andrew hoisted the sail
  and Peter took the helm.

Jesus was tired after being awake
  since well before dawn.

He had also climbed up
  into the quiet hills to pray.

The sun glinted on the water,
  and a light breeze gently rocked them
  back and forth.
  It wasn't long before Jesus
  nodded off to sleep.
  Suddenly, out of nowhere,
  a fierce wind blew up.

The sea churned and boiled
  angrily, and the boat
  rolled and tossed
  on the waves,

up   up
  and   and
    down,   down.

Jesus didn't seem bothered
by the weather.

But He looked lovingly
at their anxious faces
and stood up
in the bow of the boat.

In a firm, calm voice
He spoke to the raging sea.
"Be still!"
ordered Jesus.
All at once,
the wind started to relax
and became gentle again.

The sea settled down
and lapped quietly
around the boat.

The lake was once more
at peace.

The fishermen were amazed.

"Who on earth can this man be?"
they asked each other.

"Even the wind
and waves obey Him."

Another time, after Jesus
had spent all day
healing and teaching
in the hills,
He sent His friends
on ahead
in the boat.

He went off on His own
to pray.

He could see them out on the lake,
   battling against a strong wind.

Jesus started to walk out to them,
   walking on the water.

When they saw Him,
   they got quite scared.

"It's...it's...a g-g-ghost!"
   cried Andrew.

He had never seen anyone
   walking on water before.

"Don't be afraid," called Jesus,
   waving to them. "It's only Me!"

Peter wasn't so sure.

"If it really is You," he said,
   "let me come and walk to You
   on the water."

Jesus smiled.
   "Come on, then,"
   He answered.

Peter climbed out of the boat
   rather gingerly,
   looking at Jesus
   all the time.

It was amazing —
   he found himself
   walking on the sea!

Soon the Sea of Galilee
was silent and empty again,
calm and peaceful under the stars.

It seemed contented and happy.

Perhaps it knew
that Jesus was God — and, after all,
it was God who made the wind
and the sea.

Note:
This story is found
in Matthew 14:22-33,
Mark 4:35-41 and 6:45-56
and John 6:16-21.

Then he started to panic.
"Suppose I sink," he thought nervously.

Sure enough,
he started to drop
down
down
into the water.

"Help!" shouted Peter. "Help! I'm drowning."

Quick as a flash,
Jesus' strong arms were there
to hold him and pull him out.

Together they went
back to the boat and climbed in.

"You didn't trust Me enough, you see,"
Jesus told Peter.
"That's why you started to sink."

Strangely enough,
now that Jesus was with them,
the wind seemed friendly again.

They reached the other side
of the sea in no time.

Martha, Mary and Jesus

How Jesus must have loved that Bethany family! And how they must have loved Him. Christians who serve others still show their love for Jesus.

Martha and Mary were sisters.
  They lived in Bethany,
  a small village
  not far from Jerusalem.

Martha and Mary
  were very good
  friends of Jesus,
  so you can imagine
  how pleased they were
  when He came one day
  to visit them at their home.

"Hello, Jesus," said Mary, running out
  to meet Him. "It's so good to see You!"

Martha stood in the doorway,
  watching. She thought,
  "I must tidy the house
  and get some food ready!"

While Martha worked hard
  in the house,
  Mary sat with Jesus
  in the little garden.

Jesus had a lot
  to talk about!
  He wanted to tell them
  all He knew about God,
  His Father in heaven.
  He wanted them to know
  how much God loves
  all His people.

Mary sat quietly and listened
  and listened!

She loved to hear Jesus
  speak like this,
  and she tried to remember
  everything He said.

Some time later,
Martha and Mary's brother,
Lazarus, fell ill.

Martha and Mary
were very worried
about him,
and they sent
a messenger
to find Jesus.

"Please see if you
can find Jesus,
and tell Him
that Lazarus
is very ill.
Hurry, please!"
they told the messenger.

Martha came out of the house,
all hot and bothered!
"Jesus," she said,
"I have been working so hard!
Please tell Mary to come and help me!"

But Jesus replied,
"Martha, I know you have
been working very hard.
But what I had to say
was so important that
Mary was right to
stop and listen!
Let's just have a simple meal
and enjoy our time together."

So Mary and Martha spent a restful,
happy day with Jesus,
their very special friend.

The messenger found Jesus
with some of His other friends,
and gave Him the message.

Jesus' friends expected
Him to leave at once.
But He didn't.

The friends were puzzled,
but Jesus knew exactly
what He was doing.

He waited for two days before leaving.
"Let's go now to see Lazarus,"
He said, much to the relief
of His friends.

But they hadn't even reached Bethany
when word came
that Lazarus had died.

When they reached the house,
it was already full of friends who had
come to comfort Martha and Mary.
"We are so very sad that Lazarus has died,"
they said.
Mary stayed at home, crying
because she was so sad.

But Martha went out to meet Jesus:
"Oh Jesus, if only You had been here,
our brother would not have died!
But I know that You can help him,
even now."

Jesus understood how sad she felt.
He said, "Do you believe
that I am the Son of God?"

Trying not to cry, Martha said,
"Yes, Jesus, I do!"

Then Martha went to get Mary,
and together they met Jesus
and their friends.

"Where have you buried Lazarus?" asked Jesus.
"Come with us and we will
show You," they said.

So Martha, Mary and their friends
went with Jesus
to the tomb where Lazarus had been buried.
They were all very upset.

One of the people said, "Jesus gave sight
to the blind man, didn't He?
So perhaps He could have made Lazarus well."
When they reached the tomb,
which was carved out
of a rock in the hillside,
Jesus said, "Take the stone away!"

And two of the strongest men heaved the stone away
from the front of the tomb.

Then everyone was quiet
as Jesus prayed to God, His Father in heaven:
"Thank You, Father, for hearing My prayers.
Please help Me to show these people that it was You
who sent Me to earth to tell them about Your love."

When He had finished praying, Jesus said
in a loud voice, "Lazarus, come out!"
And Lazarus did!
Everyone gasped!
They could hardly believe what they saw!
"How wonderful," they said.
"Thanks to Jesus, the Son of God,
Lazarus is alive again!"

Jesus had shown them what God's love can do.
He had also promised
that those who love God
and believe in Jesus
are given new life forever.

Some time later,
  Jesus went again
  to Bethany to visit
  Martha, Mary and Lazarus.

Mary and Martha had prepared
  a lovely meal for them all,
  and they had invited
  some other guests, too.

They all sat around
  the table, listening
  to Jesus and enjoying
  the good food.

Jesus was enjoying Himself
  tremendously! He always
  liked being with His friends,
  and they always thought
  He was very good company!

This time, He was especially
  pleased to see His friend
  Lazarus looking happy and well.

During the meal, the sisters
  were kept very busy.
  They were filling up the plates
  and bustling about,
  making sure that everyone
  had plenty to eat and drink.

When the meal was over,
  the guests felt happy and contented.
  "That was a lovely meal," they said.

They were all surprised
  to see what Mary did next.

For a long time, Mary
  had been wanting to show
  Jesus how much she loved Him.
  She had spent all her savings
  on some very expensive perfume.
  To show how much
  she loved her special friend,
  she poured the perfume
  on Jesus' feet.

Then Mary wiped Jesus' feet
  with her hair.
  The perfume filled the air
  with a lovely fragrance.

But one of the guests said angrily,
  "What a waste of money!
  You should have spent it
  on something more important —
  like buying food
  for the poor people!"

But Jesus said,
  "Don't blame Mary!
  It is important to look after
  the poor people, but
  Mary knows that I will soon
  go to My Father in heaven.
  By giving Me this special gift
  she is showing how much
  she loves Me and My Father.
  This is very important, too!"

Note:
This story is found in
Luke 10:38-42 and
John 11:1 – 12:11.

The Wedding Feast

God offers us the best invitation of all — eternal life with Him. Jesus used a story to show why we need to accept God's calling.

Jesus often told stories
  to help His friends
  understand how much
  God loves us all.

This is one of the stories
  Jesus told.

Once there was a king
  who was getting ready
  for his son's wedding.

In the palace,
  everyone was talking
  about the happy couple,
  and what a lovely wedding
  it would be.

When everything was ready
  for the wedding feast,
  Nechemiah, the king's steward
  (who liked
  telling people what to do!),
  got out his list of people
  who had been invited.

Importantly, he read out
  all the names,
  and the servants
  went off to visit
  each one.

The first servant went
  to Theo's house.
  "The wedding feast is ready,"
  he said.
  "The king is waiting to welcome you!"

But Theo said,
  "I'm sorry, but I won't
  be able to come after all.
  It's a very busy time on the farm,
  and I have many things
  to do. Please give
  the king my apologies."

The third servant went
  to find Danny on his farm.
  "The wedding feast is ready," he said.
  "The king is waiting
  to welcome you!"

But Danny said,
  "I'm sorry, but I won't
  be able to come after all.
  I haven't fed my oxen yet,
  and their stall needs
  a good cleaning, too.
  Please give the king
  my apologies."

The second servant went
  to Will's house.
  "The wedding feast is ready," he said.
  "The king is waiting
  to welcome you!"

But Will said,
  "I'm sorry, but I won't
  be able to come after all.
  I have just moved
  into this new shop,
  and there is such
  a lot to do.
  Please give my apologies
  to the king."

42

They searched the streets,
  and asked all who were deaf, lame
  or blind if they would like to come to
  the wedding of the king's son.
  The people who were deaf, lame
  or blind were very pleased!
  They tidied themselves up
  and went to the palace.

Then the servants looked up and down
  the alleyways, in and out of houses.
  They ran here and there, searching far
  and wide, asking all the poor people
  they could find:
  "Would you like to come
  to the wedding of the king's son?"

The fourth servant went to Tobias' house.
  "The wedding feast is ready," he said.
  "The king is waiting to welcome you!"

"Go away!" said Tobias. "It hasn't been long
  since my own wedding and I'm far too busy
  to come to the wedding of the king's son!
  Tell the king I would come if I could!"

One by one,
  the servants told the king the excuses
  that the guests had made for not being able
  to come to the wedding feast after all.
  The king was very mad.

"But everything is ready," he said.
  "We must have some guests!
  Go out into the streets
  and invite anybody
  you can find —
  bring in the poor,
  the deaf, the lame
  and the blind!"

The servants ran off
  in all directions.

43

The servants ran off to the country
  as fast as they could.
  They searched all the fields
  and orchards;
  all the roads and hedges;
  behind the trees
  and in the ditches!

They looked far and wide,
  high and low.
  (By this time they were
  getting very tired!)

They invited everyone
  they could find to the wedding feast.

The poor people
  were very pleased!
  They also cleaned themselves up
  and went to the palace.

The servants went back to see the king.
  "Well done!" said the king.
  "We have lots of guests now,
  but there are still some empty places.
  Go out into the countryside
  and find more people
  to come to the feast.
  I want my house to be full.
  If the people I invited
  are making excuses
  to stay away, I will look
  for others who want
  to come!"

Back at the palace,
  the king was looking
  happier and happier.

All the seats were filled with people,
  and the food on the table
  looked delicious!

Though many of them
  were very poor,
  the people had tried hard
  to look their best.
  They had brushed their hair,
  washed their faces,
  and tidied themselves up
  in honor of the wedding
  of the king's son.

The only thing that upset
  the king now was that one of the guests
  had made no effort to tidy himself up.

His hair was a mess,
  his clothes were dirty
  and he looked
  as if he couldn't care less.

The king sent that man away.

The crowd who had gathered
  to hear Jesus speak
  liked the story very much.
  But, of course,
  they wanted to know
  what it meant.

Jesus explained
  that the king was like
  God, our Father in heaven.
  He invites people to His house,
  because He loves them.
  The people who love God
  will come when He calls;
  they won't make excuses!
  He invites all of us —
  will you come?

Note:
This story is found
in Luke 14:15-26
and Matthew 22:1-14.

The Secret on the Mountain

When Jesus talks about giving
His life to save the world,
everything about Him shines.
This is the secret.

If you had lived in Galilee
about 2,000 years ago,
you would probably have met
Jesus at work.

He spent a lot of time
making people better,
talking with them and teaching them
how to love one another.

Often, in the evening,
or before the sun came up,
Jesus set off by Himself
into the mountains, to spend some time
with God, His Father.

It was so peaceful.
The moon and the planets,
and all the distant stars,
are there because God has made them.

And Jesus, standing on Earth,
could share God's love, which made it all.

(His love still keeps it going, even today!)

Sometimes Jesus would say
a thank-You to His Father
for the wonders of His world.

Sometimes He talked to God
about the people He loved
and about their needs.

And sometimes He just stood quietly,
happy to be in God's company.

"You can borrow my staff
if you like," said John, kindly.

"Think of the view we'll have
at the top!" said James.

The view was fantastic.
All the hills and valleys
were stretched out
far below, in the sunlight.

There were tiny clusters
of houses and trees.
And the lake glinted,
clear and blue,
with dots of boats
moving across it.

"Isn't God's world beautiful?"
whispered James.

Jesus smiled.
"It certainly is!" He agreed.

One day Jesus asked
three of His friends
to climb the mountain with Him.
"But don't You need some time
on Your own, Jesus?" they asked.

"Not today," Jesus said.
"I'd like you to come as well."
James, John and Peter
were very pleased to be asked.

Together, they started to climb.
The path was steep and rocky.
Lizards blinked at them,
and the dust felt gritty
in their sandals.

Peter was out of breath.
"Phew!" he gasped,
mopping his head with his sleeve.
"Are we nearly at the top?"

Jesus was talking with them
  about how He would save the world
  by dying for it,
  before coming to life again forever.

"We are being allowed
  to look into heaven!" thought John.
  It made him feel very peaceful
  and very happy.

Peter wanted to hold on
  to this moment forever.
  "What a good thing we're here,
  Master," he said.
  "We could make three shelters —
  one for each of you!"

Then Jesus began to pray.
  He prayed with such love
  and such joy
  that His face was lit up
  and radiantly happy.

Peter, James and John
  watched Him in amazement.
  They had never seen anyone
  pray like this before.

As they gazed at Jesus
  they saw God's light
  spread through His whole body.
  Everything about Him shone.

Two men were standing
  with Him now.
  They were Moses and Elijah
  (who had both been
  faithful to God
  during their lifetimes).

48

John, Peter and James
could hardly take in
what was happening.
The wonder of it all
made them frightened.

(After all, it's not every day that
you see the secrets of heaven!)

They clung to each other,
terrified.

Just then,
a bright cloud settled
on the mountain.

Out of the cloud
came a voice,
more powerful
— and yet more gentle —
than any voice
they had ever heard.

Yes, it was the voice
of God Himself.

"This is My dear Son,"
He said.
"I'm very pleased with Him.
Listen to what He tells you."

Jesus walked over
and put His arm
around their shoulders.
He looked normal now,
and Moses and Elijah had gone.

"Don't be afraid,"
said Jesus, softly.

"Please, Jesus, cure my daughter!"

"Jesus, my mother is ill —
   can You help?"

"Jesus, my son has fits,
   and Your friends
   can't heal him.
   Will You make him better?"

Very soon, Jesus was back
   working among the people He loved.
   No wonder God had said
   He was pleased with His Son.

Peter, James and John
   never forgot the shining majesty
   of Jesus on that mountain.

The disciples were itching to tell
   everyone what they had seen.
   Jesus had other ideas.

As they scrambled down
   the steep mountain trail,
   He said to them,
   "I don't want you to tell
   anyone this secret yet;
   wait until I have come
   back to life again.
   Then you can tell
   whoever you like."

After seeing the light of heaven
   on the mountain,
   it was strange to see
   flustered crowds
   gathered in the valley.
   They all needed Jesus
   and felt lost without Him.

And they kept their promise:
   they didn't tell anyone
   the secret until after Jesus
   had come back to life.

(And one day,
   at the end of time,
   we will ALL see Him
   in His shining glory!)

Note:
This story is found in
Matthew 17:1-9; Mark 9:2-9;
Luke 9:28-36 and 2 Peter 1:16-18.

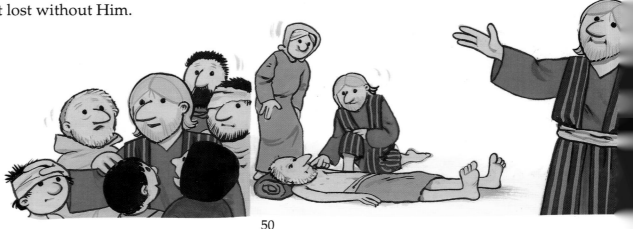

Peter in Prison

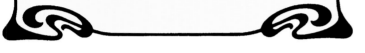

"I thought I was dreaming," we say when something marvelous has happened to us. What God has planned for us is like a dream.

Herod's soldiers found Peter in the city and arrested him.

People were getting ready for the Feast of the Passover (when they remembered their people's escape to freedom from Egypt). Everyone watched sadly as the soldiers told Peter what Herod had ordered. They had come to take Peter to prison.

King Herod was very powerful. He ruled over Galilee, Judea and Samaria.

He hated the followers of Jesus, and did his best to make things as difficult for them as he could.

One day, when he was in a really bad mood, he decided that James, one of Jesus' close friends, should be killed.

Poor James was taken away by Herod's soldiers.

Not content with this, Herod sent his soldiers to look for Peter, too.

Peter had been a fisherman when he first met Jesus, and had become one of Jesus' most loyal friends.

When Peter's friends
   heard that he was in prison,
   they were very unhappy.

They knew that Herod
   did not like them
   because they were Jesus' friends,
   but they did not expect him
   to be so unkind.

They all prayed
   as hard as they could,
   asking God to look after Peter
   and to help him.

Peter tried to sleep.
   It was very difficult,
   as he was bound with chains
   and felt uncomfortable.
   He was sad and lonely,
   but he went on trusting God.
   At last, he nodded off and slept.

The guards were bored.
   They stood chatting
   about what they would do
   when their night's duty ended.

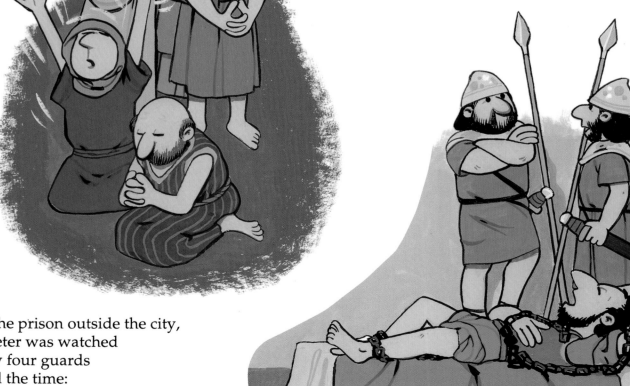

In the prison outside the city,
   Peter was watched
   by four guards
   all the time:
   two stood by the door
   and two stood beside his bed.

Peter was sleepy,
    dazed and amazed.
    He couldn't believe
    what was happening!

The chains fell from
    Peter's wrists and ankles,
    and he got ready
    just as the angel had said.

"Follow me, Peter,"
    said the angel.

And Peter did —
    though he thought
    he was dreaming!

"Can this be true?"
    he wondered.

"Is it really happening
    to me?"

It wasn't long before
    a lovely, gentle light
    flooded the prison cell,
    and an angel of God appeared.

(The soldiers went on talking,
    since they could not see
    the angel.)

The angel tapped Peter
    on the shoulder
    and then beckoned to him.

"Get up, Peter," he said.

"Hurry! Pick up your sandals,
    fasten your belt,
    put on your cloak
    and follow me!"

The angel led the way,
    smiling at the sight
    of Peter's puzzled face.

They walked past the first guard post,
    and then the second…

After a while,
    they came to the gate
    leading into the city.

To Peter's surprise
    (he still thought he was dreaming)
    the gate opened by itself!

The angel and Peter
    walked through the gate
    and on down the street.

Suddenly, without a word,
    the angel left Peter,
    and disappeared altogether.

The truth dawned on Peter at last!
    "Now I know what has
    happened," he said.
    "The Lord sent His angel
    to rescue me from Herod's power,
    and he has set me free from prison.
    How wonderful!"

He was so delighted
    and relieved,
    he wanted to see his friends,
    and tell them the good news.

Peter went straight
  to Mary's house
  where he knew
  some of his friends would be.
  (You probably remember
  that Jesus' mother
  was named Mary;
  the Mary in this story
  was not Jesus' mother,
  but the mother of John Mark.)

He knocked at the door
  and called out.

Rhoda, a servant girl,
  came to see who was there.
  As soon as Rhoda
  heard Peter's voice,
  she knew who it was.
  She was so excited
  that she didn't even
  open the door!

Instead, she rushed back
  into the room.
  "Peter is at the door!"
  she cried.

Peter's friends knew that he was in prison,
  so they thought Rhoda must be crazy —
  or imagining things —
  or something!

They said, "Don't be silly, Rhoda!
  It can't be Peter!"

Meanwhile, Peter was still
  standing outside the door,
  wondering what was happening!
  He knocked again.

Eventually, the friends
  decided to go and look for themselves.

They opened the door and saw
  — it *was* Peter!

They were surprised, and very pleased.

The next morning,
  when the guards found
  that Peter had gone,
  there was uproar
  and confusion!

They searched high and low,
  but there was no sign
  of their prisoner.

And when he heard the news
  Herod was absolutely FURIOUS
  — as you might have guessed!

But by this time,
  Peter was safe,
  and a long way away.

Note:
This story is found
in Acts 12:1-19.

They all went together
  into the house to celebrate.
  But Peter had other things to do.

Gently, he asked his friends
  to be quiet and listen.
  (They had been talking
  and laughing with delight!)

When they were quiet,
  he told them how the Lord
  had sent His angel
  to rescue him from prison.

Then it was time for him to go.
  As he left the house he said,
  "Please tell James
  and the other friends of Jesus
  what has happened."

Wind & Fire

Far from being dead, Jesus is more alive than ever in people who have His Spirit and begin to live as He did.

Ever since Jesus died,
  Peter had felt kind of lost.
  He knew Jesus was alive again —
  after all, he had seen Him.

But Jesus wasn't with them
  all the time any more,
  and Peter really missed Him.

He kicked a stone.
  "Oh, let's go fishing,"
  he muttered to his friends.

Guess how many fish they caught?
  None!

When morning came,
  a man on the beach
  called to them,
  "Try your nets
  on the other side!"

Well, now they found so many fish
  the nets could hardly hold them.

"That man on the beach
  must be Jesus!"
  shouted John,
  and Peter dived in and swam ashore
  to get to Him faster.

Happily, they all had
  a lovely breakfast together.

It swept through the room
and seemed to settle, brightly,
on each person like flames of fire.

It felt as if Jesus
was not just with them, now,
but actually alive —
like a warm glow
inside of them!

They were so excited,
and so happy,
that they rushed out of the house,
singing, dancing and
praising God with all their might.

One day Jesus met His friends again.
"It's time for Me to go back to My Father,
in heaven now," He explained,
"but I will send you My Spirit;
then I will be with you all the time,
wherever you are."

They watched as Jesus was taken
into heaven.
Then they walked home
and waited hopefully
for Jesus to keep His promise.

A week later,
they were praying together
when a sound like the wind
began to roar through the house.
They could feel its power.

58

Peter heard him,
  but he was too happy
  to be angry.
  He said,
  "No, sir, we're not drunk!"

Peter told the people
  that when they had
  crucified Jesus,
  they had crucified God;
  but God had raised Jesus
  to life again.

The people were horrified.

"What can we do, Peter?"
  they asked.

"Tell God you are sorry,
  and then be baptized
  in Jesus' name,"
  said Peter.

Neighbors and visiting pilgrims
  heard the noise of the wind
  and stopped to see
  what was going on.

Jerusalem was full of visitors
  from other countries,
  and they all spoke
  different languages,
  of course.

The odd thing was
  that everybody could understand
  what Peter and the others
  were talking about.

Full of joy and wonder,
  they were telling everyone
  about what Jesus had done,
  and how He was God's own Son.
  And the people could understand
  every word.

"They've had too much to drink!"
  sneered one man.

After that,
  Peter and the others
  were kept very busy,
  baptizing many people —
  they baptized 3,000
  people that day.

What a wonderful day!

They joyfully praised their Lord,
  and asked for His help
  and guidance.

Together they shared their meals
  and broke bread,
  as Jesus had done.

They were called
  "followers of the Way."
  Every day
  more people joined them.

The believers wanted to live
  Jesus' way — the loving way.
  They sold their belongings
  and shared everything.

"Stop talking about Jesus
  as if He is alive,"
  they demanded.
  "We know He's dead.
  And He was wrong to pretend
  He was God's Son."

"But He *is* alive!"
  said Peter, "And He *is* God's Son!"

"Look," said the man who
  wasn't crippled anymore.
  "Jesus just healed these legs of mine!"

But Peter and John
  were thrown into prison for the night.

One day,
  on their way to the temple,
  Peter and John saw a man
  who couldn't walk,
  sitting and begging.
  "We have no silver or gold," said Peter,
  "but I will gladly share
  what I do have."

He looked lovingly at the man.
  "In the name of Jesus,"
  he said, "get up and walk!"

Peter held the man's hand
  to help him up.

The man sprang to his feet.
  He found he could walk!
  He could jump!
  He could run!

When the people saw him
  leaping about, praising God,
  they were amazed.

"But that man's a cripple!"
  they said.

"Not anymore, I'm not!"
  laughed the man.

Just then the chief priests
  arrived, furious.

By now
  there were 5,000
  followers of the Way —
  good news travels fast!

Peter, John and the others
  were often thrown into prison,
  or beaten, to try to keep them
  from spreading the news
  about Jesus.

But nothing and no one
  could ever stop their
  telling the people
  what they knew was true:

"Jesus is God's Son,
  He's ALIVE
  and He loves us!"

Note:
This story is found in
John 21:1-14
and Acts 2:1 – 4:4.